# I WONDER Why

# The Wind Blows

and other questions
about our planet

Anita Ganeri

KINGFISHER

NEW YORK

# CONTENTS

4   Is Earth round?

5   What is Earth made of?

6   How old is Earth?

7   Has Earth changed much?

8   Where are the
    highest mountains?

9   Can mountains
    shrink?

10   Which mountains breathe fire?

11   Do people live on volcanoes?

12   What makes Earth shake?

13   Can people tell if an earthquake
     is coming?

14   What is the Room of Candles?

15   What's the difference between
     stalactites and stalagmites?

16   Where do rivers begin?

16   Why do old rivers flow so slowly?

17   Where do rivers end?

18   How high is the sky?

18   What is the greenhouse effect?

20 What are clouds made of?

20 When does rain fall
 from clouds?

21 How cold is snow?

22 Where do thunderstorms
 start?

23 What is thunder?

24 What is a tornado?

25 Why does the wind blow?

26 When does it rain in
 a rainforest?

26 Where are rainforests?

27 Where is the biggest forest?

28 Where does it never rain?

29 Which is the
 sandiest desert?

29 How hot are deserts?

30 What's it like at
 the poles?

30 Which is the coldest place
 in the world?

31 Where do polar
 bears live?

32 Index

# Is Earth round?

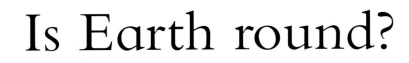

If you were an astronaut floating around in space, Earth would look like a gigantic ball. It isn't perfectly round, though. Like a ball that's been gently squashed, it's slightly flatter at the top and bottom, and it bulges out just a little in the middle.

Equator

Earth measures 24,900 miles (40,075km) around its "waist"— the equator. If you walked night and day, it would take you more than a year to travel that distance!

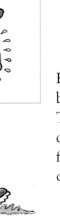

Earth looks blue from space. That's because almost three-fourths of it is covered by the sea.

The crust is the rocky layer beneath your feet.

The mantle is a thick layer of rock. It's so hot that some of the rock has melted.

The core is made of metal. The outer core is runny and liquid, but the inner core is solid.

Outer core

Inner core

It's very hot at the center of Earth—more than 9,000°F (5,000°C). For comparison, a really hot summer's day can be 85–100°F (30–40°C).

# What is Earth made of?

Earth is made up of different layers of rock and metal. Some of the layers are hard, but others are so hot that they've melted and are runny—a little like hot, sticky caramel.

Earth's crust doesn't stop at the seashore. It continues under the deepest oceans.

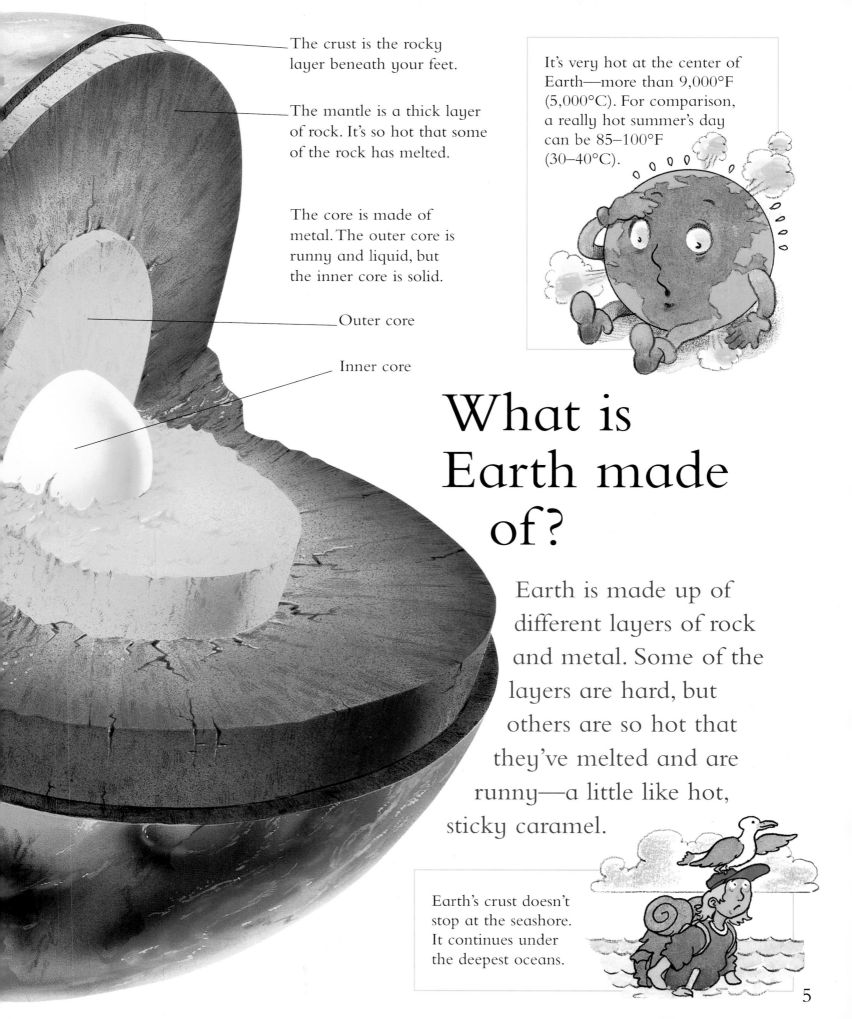

# How old is Earth?

Scientists think that Earth formed about 4.6 billion years ago—although no one was there to see it! They think the Moon formed then, too.

Human beings are very new to Earth. If you imagine our planet's 4.6-billion-year history squeezed into one year, people have been around only since late on December 31!

About 200 million years ago, there was just one super-continent called Pangaea.

**Pangaea**

About 180 million years ago, Pangaea began to break up.

Continents are massive pieces of land. There are seven of them in all. Trace them from a map and try to see how they once fit together.

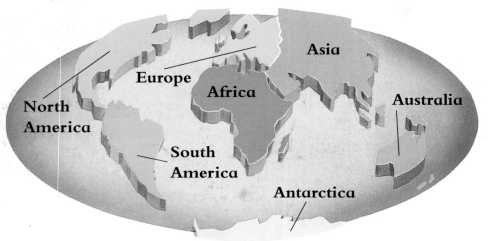

Asia
Europe
Africa
Australia
North America
South America
Antarctica

Emus live in Australia, rheas in South America, and ostrich in Africa. They look similar, and none of them can fly. They may once have been related to one kind of bird. It could have walked to all three continents millions of years ago, when the land was connected.

# Has Earth changed much?

Yes, it has! About 200 million years ago, most of the land was joined together in one big piece. Then it began to break up into smaller pieces called continents. These slowly drifted apart, until they reached the places they're in today.

About 65 million years ago, the continents drifted farther apart.

Today, the continents are still drifting.

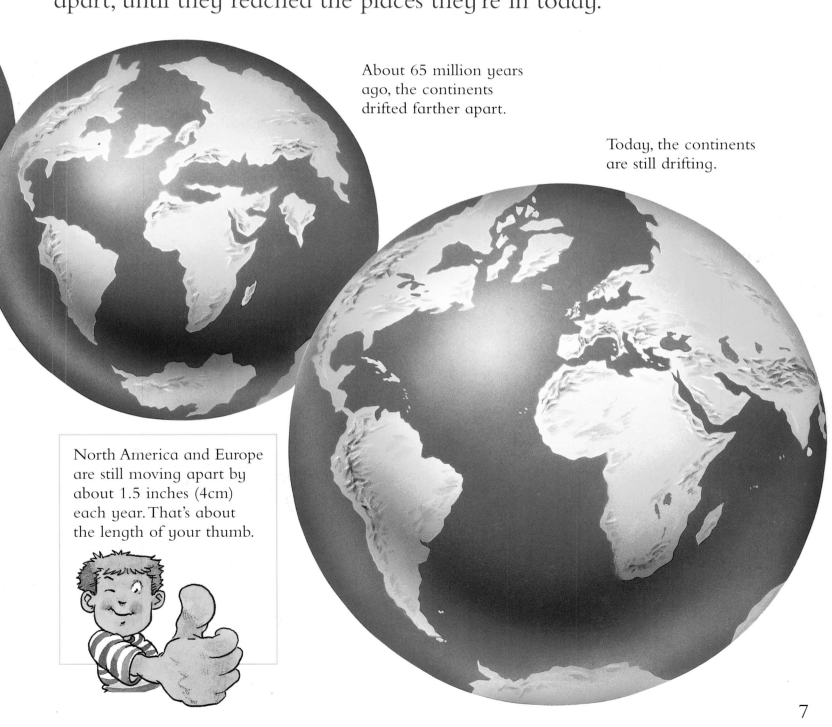

North America and Europe are still moving apart by about 1.5 inches (4cm) each year. That's about the length of your thumb.

# Where are the highest mountains?

The Himalayas in Asia are the world's highest mountains. They're so high that they're known as the "roof of the world." The towering mountain peaks are bitterly cold places, where the snow and ice never melt.

*Himalaya* means "home of the snows." It's a good name for these freezing peaks.

These are the highest mountains in each continent:

Asia—Mt. Everest 29,029 ft. (8,848m)

South America—Aconcagua 22,831 ft. (6,959m)

North America—Mt. McKinley 20,322 ft. (6,194m)

Africa—Mt. Kilimanjaro 19,341 ft. (5,895m)

Europe—Mt. Elbrus 18,481 ft. (5,633m)

Antarctica—Vinson Massif 16,050 ft. (4,892m)

Australia—Mt. Kosciuszko 7,316 ft. (2,230m)

# Can mountains shrink?

Many mountains are getting smaller all the time. Every day, small chips of rock are carried away by ice, snow, and running water. Some mountains are getting bigger, though. The Himalayas are still being pushed up by movements inside of Earth.

In Hawaii, there is a mountain called Mauna Kea that is 4,265 feet (1,300m) taller than Mount Everest. Most of it is under the sea, though.

The higher you go up a mountain, the colder it becomes. Many of the animals that live up on mountains have thick, woolly coats to keep out the cold— goats, llamas, and yaks, for example.

# Which mountains breathe fire?

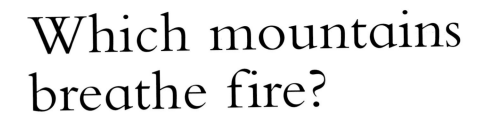

Volcanoes are mountains that sometimes spurt out burning ash, gas, and hot, runny rock called lava. The gas and fiery lava come from deep down inside of Earth and burst up through cracks in the crust.

The saucerlike top of a volcano is called a crater. Sometimes a dead volcano's crater fills with rainwater and makes a beautiful lake.

There are about 500 active volcanoes on land. There are even more under the sea.

# Do people live on volcanoes?

It's a risky thing to do, but many people live on volcanoes—especially farmers. The ash from a volcano makes the soil very rich, so the farmers can grow bumper crops. They might need to be able to run fast, though!

There are volcanoes in space, too. Olympus Mons on the planet Mars is three times higher than Earth's Mount Everest.

Pilots beware! The ash and dust from a volcano can get inside a plane's engines and stop them dead.

# What makes Earth shake?

Earth's surface is made up of huge pieces of hard rock that drift on the hot, runny rock below. Sometimes these pieces push and shove against each other, causing Earth to shake. This is what happens during an earthquake.

In the worst earthquakes, the ground cracks open, streets sink, and buildings crumble into piles of rubble.

The greatest danger during an earthquake is a building collapsing on top of you. Sheltering under a table or a doorway may save your life.

# Can people tell if an earthquake is coming?

Scientists who study earthquakes are called seismologists. Although they know where earthquakes are likely to happen, they usually can't say exactly when.

People have tried to design earthquake-proof buildings. Some of the latest ones are shaped like pyramids or cones.

Animals seem to feel the land moving long before people do. Dogs howl, snakes wriggle out of their holes, and chickens run for their lives!

The people of ancient China believed that Earth was balanced on the shoulders of a giant ox. Earthquakes happened when the ox shifted Earth from one shoulder to the other.

# What is the Room of Candles?

Deep down below the mountain slopes of eastern Italy is a magical cave known as the Room of Candles. It gets its name from the white spikes of rock that grow up from the floor of the cave, like candles. They are really stalagmites, and they grow in small cups of rock that look like candleholders.

Like all underground caves, the Room of Candles was made by rainwater trickling down and eating away at the rock.

Thousands of years ago, people sheltered in caves. They painted pictures of bison and woolly mammoths on the walls.

People who like to explore the secret world of underground tunnels and caves are called spelunkers or cavers.

Bats love the darkness of caves. They roost in them during the daytime, and they use them as nurseries for their babies.

Don't sit and watch a stalactite grow. It can take more than 1,000 years to get less than half an inch (1cm) longer!

# What's the difference between stalactites and stalagmites?

Stalactites and stalagmites are both long and pointed, like icicles made of rock. The only difference between them is that while stalactites grow down from the roof of a cave, stalagmites grow up from the floor.

Who lives in dark underground caves? Lizards and worms—that's who!

# Where do rivers begin?

Rivers start as tiny streams. Some streams start where springs bubble out of the ground. Others form on mountains, when the tips of icy glaciers begin to melt. And some trickle out of lakes.

On some mountains, huge rivers of ice grind slowly downhill. These ice rivers are called glaciers.

**1.** Rain falls on the hills and sinks into the ground.

**2.** Water trickles up out of a spring.

**3.** The stream joins others and becomes a fast-flowing river.

**4.** The river reaches flatter land. It gets wider and flows more slowly.

# Why do old rivers flow so slowly?

At the bottom of a hill, the ground becomes flatter, slowing the river down. Instead of rushing downhill in a straight line, the river flows in big bends called meanders.

# Where do rivers end?

Most rivers end their journey at the sea. The mouth of the river is where fresh river water mixes with the salty water of the sea.

The longest river in the world is the Nile River, which goes through Egypt. It flows for 4,145 miles (6,670km).

Some rivers don't flow into the sea. They flow into lakes instead, or they drain into the ground.

The world's shortest river is the D River in Oregon. At just 120 feet (37m), it is only about as long as ten canoes.

**5.** A river sometimes cuts through one of its bends—leaving behind a curvy oxbow lake.

Birds love feeding at the mouth of a river. They pull out the worms that live in the gooey mud!

**6.** At its mouth, the river joins the salty water of the sea.

17

# How high is the sky?

The sky is part of an invisible skin of air around Earth. This skin is called the atmosphere, and it reaches out into space for about 300 miles (500km). There's a very important gas called oxygen in the atmosphere—we all need to breathe oxygen to stay alive.

Earth is the only planet known to have enough oxygen for living things.

If Earth gets too hot, the ice at the poles could melt. The seas would rise and drown many towns along the coasts.

# What is the greenhouse effect?

The greenhouse effect is the name that scientists have given to a hot problem. Waste gases from factories, power plants, and cars are building up in the atmosphere and trapping too much heat close to Earth. Our planet is slowly getting warmer—like a greenhouse in the summer.

**OZONE LAYER**

**3.** Above where planes fly is the ozone layer. It works a little like a sunscreen, protecting us from the Sun's burning rays.

**2.** Planes fly in the next layer, high above the clouds, where the skies are clear. The air is thinner here and has less oxygen in it.

**1.** The atmosphere is made up of different layers. In the lowest layer, the air carries clouds and weather around Earth.

# What are clouds made of?

Some clouds look like they're made of cotton balls—but they're not! Clouds are made up of billions of water droplets and ice crystals. These are so tiny and light that they float in the air.

Without rain, no plants would grow. Then what would we all eat?

You would need your umbrella on Mount Wai'ale'ale in Hawaii. It rains there for 350 days each year.

# When does rain fall from clouds?

Rain falls when water droplets in a cloud start joining together. They get bigger and heavier until, in the end, they are too heavy to float, and they fall to the ground as rain.

Have you ever heard of showers of frogs or fish? Well, they do happen. These animals are sometimes sucked up from ponds by extrastrong winds. Later, they fall to the ground with the rain.

# How cold is snow?

Snowflakes are water droplets that have frozen into crystals of ice. To stay frozen, they have to be at freezing point—that's 32°F (0°C). If they get any warmer than that, snowflakes melt and fall to the ground as rain.

How big can you build a snowman? The tallest ever constructed was 122 feet (37m) high—and was actually a snowwoman.

# Where do thunderstorms start?

Thunderstorms start in the huge black thunderclouds that sometimes gather at the end of a hot summer's day. Inside the clouds, strong winds hurl the water droplets around, and the cloud crackles with electricity. This flashes through the sky in great dazzling sparks, which we call lightning.

It's safest to stay inside during a thunderstorm. Never shelter under a tree—it might get struck by lightning.

An American man was struck by lightning seven times! Roy C. Sullivan had his hair set alight twice and his eyebrows burned off. He even lost a big toenail.

Lightning can travel as far as 87,000 miles (140,000km) in one second flat!

To find out how far away a storm is, count the number of seconds between the lightning and the thunder. The storm is one mile (1.6km) away for every five seconds you count.

The biggest thunderclouds tower 10 miles (16km) into the air. That's almost twice the height of Mount Everest.

# What is thunder?

Sparks of lightning are incredibly hot. As they flash through the sky, they heat the air so quickly that it makes a loud booming noise like an explosion. This is thunder.

# What is a tornado?

A tornado is a spinning twist of wind that speeds across the ground, sucking up everything in its path. Tornadoes happen mainly in North America. Hurricanes are another kind of spinning storm, but they begin over warm tropical seas. Hurricane winds can blow at speeds of up to 150 miles per hour (240km/h).

In Minnesota, in 1931, a tornado lifted a train into the air and dumped it in a ditch.

Air is invisible, so you can't see the wind. But you can feel it on your face and see how it makes the trees sway.

# Why does the wind blow?

When you feel the wind blow, it's because air is on the move. Air moves when it's warm. It gets lighter and rises up into the sky. Cooler air then rushes in to take its place, making a breeze.

Here's proof that warm air rises. Put a feather over a hot radiator and watch it float upward on the rising air.

# When does it rain in a rainforest?

It rains almost every day in a rainforest, but it doesn't pour all day long. The air gets hotter and hotter, and stickier and stickier, until there's a heavy thunderstorm in the afternoon. After that, it's dry again.

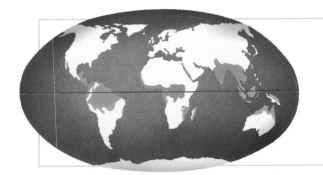

The world's biggest rainforest is in South America. It stretches for thousands of miles along the banks of the Amazon River.

# Where are rainforests?

The places where rainforests grow are shown in green on the map above. These are the world's warmest areas, close to the equator.

Anacondas are enormous snakes. They hide in the muddy waters of the Amazon, waiting for a tasty meal to pass by.

Rainforests are home to more than half of all the animals and plants that live on Earth.

This book started life as a tree trunk! Most paper comes from coniferous trees, such as spruce and pine.

# Where is the biggest forest?

The world's biggest forest stretches across the top of Europe and Asia. The trees in this forest are conifers—they have hard, narrow leaves called needles.

Brown bears and wolves live in the dark forests of the north. Reindeer shelter there during the long cold winters.

# Where does it never rain?

Deserts are the driest places in the world. In some deserts, it never rains at all. In others, there isn't any rain for months or years at a time. Deserts are very windy, too. The wind piles the sand up into big heaps called dunes.

The Atacama Desert in Chile, South America, is the world's driest desert. It had no rain for 400 years. Then, in 1971, it suddenly poured.

Many people who live in deserts are nomads. They move from place to place with their animals, looking for food and water.

The Sahara Desert covers about one-third of the whole of Africa.

# Which is the sandiest desert?

The Sahara Desert in North Africa is the biggest hot desert in the world. Huge parts of it are covered with rolling hills of sand. Desert land isn't always sandy, though. A lot of it is rocky, or covered with stones and gravel.

The highest sandcastle ever built stood more than 31 feet (9m) tall.

Sand blown by the wind can strip paint off a car like a giant sheet of sandpaper.

# How hot are deserts?

In the hottest desert, the temperature can rise to a scorching 120°F (50°C) or more, and there isn't a scrap of shade. But then it cools down and gets really cold at night.

# What's it like at the poles?

The North and South poles are at the very ends of Earth. They are freezing-cold places with bitterly cold winds. Ice and snow stretch as far as the eye can see— not the best place for a vacation!

Antarctica is a huge, ice-covered continent around the South Pole. In places, the ice is almost 3 miles (5km) thick.

# Which is the coldest place in the world?

Vostok Station is a really chilly place in Antarctica. The temperature there is usually about −72°F (−58°C), but it has dropped to −128°F (−89°C)—the coldest ever known!

Mount Erebus must be the warmest place in Antarctica. It's an active volcano!

# Where do polar bears live?

Polar bears live around the Arctic Ocean, near the North Pole. Funnily enough, they've never lived in Antarctica, although there's plenty of food and just as much snow and ice there.

Icebergs float in the sea. They were once part of rivers of ice called glaciers.

Polar bears never slip on the ice. The rough skin and hair on the soles of their feet give them extra grip.

# Index

## A

Africa 6, 29
air 18, 29, 25
Antarctica 6, 30
Asia 6, 8, 27
atmosphere 18–19
Australia 6

## C

cave animals 15
caves 14–15
clouds 19, 20–21, 22
continents 6–7, 8

## D

deserts 28–29

## E

Earth
 age of 6
 history of 6–7
 inside the 5, 10, 12
earthquakes 12–13
equator 4, 26
Europe 6, 7, 27

## F

forests 26–27

## G

glaciers 16, 31
greenhouse effect 18

## H

Himalayas 8, 9
hurricanes 24

## I

ice 8, 9, 30, 31
icebergs 31

## L

lakes 16, 17
lightning 22–23

## M

mountain animals 9
mountains 8–9, 10–11, 16

## N

North America 6, 7, 24
North Pole *see* poles

## O

oxbow lakes 17
oxygen 18, 19
ozone layer 19

## P

Pangaea 6
poles 18, 30–31

## R

rain 14, 16, 20, 21, 26, 28
rainforests 26, 27
rivers 16–17

## S

Sahara Desert 29
seas 4, 5, 9, 10, 17, 18, 24
sky 18–19
snow 8, 9, 21, 30, 31
South America 6, 26, 28
South Pole *see* poles

stalactites 14, 15
stalagmites 14, 15
streams 16
Sun 19

## T

thunder 23
thunderstorms 22–23
tornadoes 24–25

## V

volcanoes 10–11, 30

## W

wind 21, 22, 24, 25, 28, 30

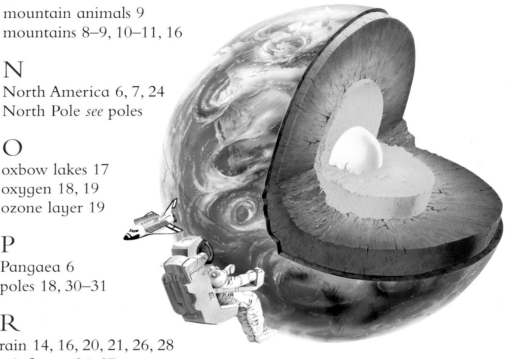

# TITLES IN THE **I WONDER WHY** SERIES

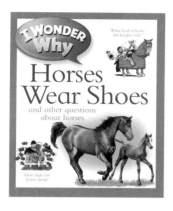

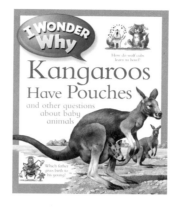

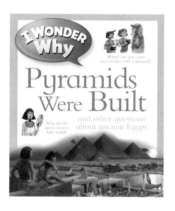

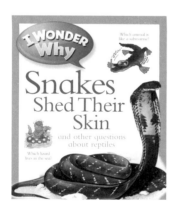

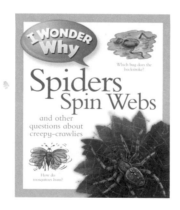

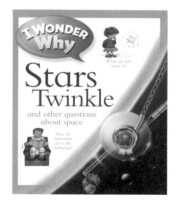

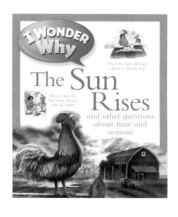

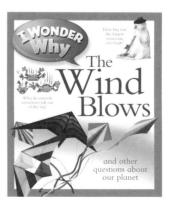